MADRID

BY DEBORAH KENT

CHILDREN'S PRESS®
A Division of Grolier Publishing
New York London Hong Kong Sydney
Danbury, Connecticut

CONSULTANTS

Elisa Baena
Madrid native
Department of Spanish
University of Illinois at Chicago

Linda Cornwell
Learning Resource Consultant
Indiana Department of Education

Project Editor: Downing Publishing Services
Design Director: Karen Kohn & Associates, Ltd.
Photo Researcher: Jan Izzo
Pronunciations: Courtesy of Tony Breed, M.A., Linguistics, University of Chicago

---

NOTES ON SPANISH PRONUNCIATION
The words in this book are pronounced basically the way the pronunciation guides look. There are a few notes, however: *ah* is like *a* in father; *ar* and *are* like *ar* in far; *ay* is as in pay; *oh, oe,* and *oa* are like *o* in hope; *oo* is as in food; *oce* is like *os* in post; *ace* is as in race; *th* is as in thing, but some people pronounce it like *s* in sing; *y* is like the *y* in yes (in some Spanish accents this sounds like the *j* in jet). There are some sounds in Spanish that do not occur in English: h̲ is like *h* as in hat, but stronger and harsher. If you try to say *k* as in kite but relax and slur the sound, it will sound like h̲.

Library of Congress Cataloging-in-Publication Data
Kent, Deborah.
 Madrid / by Deborah Kent.
  p. cm. — (Cities of the world)
 Includes bibliographical references and index.
 Summary: Describes the history, culture, daily life, food, people, sports,
and points of interest in the capital and largest city in Spain.
  ISBN 0-516-20783-0 (lib. bdg.)   0-516-26462-1 (pbk.)
  1. Madrid (Spain)—Juvenile literature. [1. Madrid (Spain)] I. Title.
II. Series: Cities of the world (New York, N.Y.)
DP354.K46 1999   98-45242
946—dc21   CIP
                           AC

TABLE OF CONTENTS

On New Year's Eve, thousands of people pack Madrid's Puerta del Sol. The Puerta del Sol is a crescent-shaped plaza in the central part of the city. It is the place where people gather to say good-bye to the old year and welcome in the new.

Puerta del Sol (PWAIR-TAH DELL SOLE)

If you are standing in the crowd, you probably clutch a small bag of grapes in your hand. Grapes play an important part in this New Year's celebration. You must not eat them until the clock strikes midnight. With each deep chime, you should pop one grape into your mouth and gobble it up. When you have eaten twelve grapes, the New Year has begun.

In English, Puerta del Sol means "Gateway of the Sun." An ancient gate once stood on this spot, adorned with a large sun carving. The gate disappeared early in the sixteenth century. But Spaniards still have a special feeling for the plaza that bears its name. They regard the Puerta del Sol as the very center of Madrid, their capital city. And Madrid lies at the center of Spain itself.

Each person celebrating New Year's Eve in the Puerta del Sol eats one grape for every chime of the clock as it strikes midnight.

Spanish information guides (in yellow) help tourists find their way around Madrid.

Madrid (MAH-DREED)

A symbol called Kilometer Zero is embedded in the square. It marks the center of Madrid—and of Spain. All distances in Spain are measured from this point in the Puerta del Sol. Madrileños like to say that all roads begin here, fanning out across the nation and the continent. They also say it in another way. The Puerta del Sol is where all roads converge. Stretching across a nation and a continent, this vast network of roads carries Madrid to the world and brings the world to the city of Madrid.

Left: Kilometer Zero, in the Puerta del Sol
Below: The Casa de Correos, on the south side of the Puerta del Sol, was once the central post office but now houses Madrid's government offices.

In the 1600s, a French woman named Madame D'Aulnoy made a long journey through Spain. At that time, Spain ruled the mightiest empire in the world. Its cities dazzled the eye with fountains, monuments, and grand cathedrals. Madame D'Aulnoy found that the people of Madrid were passionately loyal to their city. "They believe Madrid to be the very center of all glory and happiness," she wrote. "They had rather choose to lead a mean, poor life without any grandeur or distinction, provided it be but at Madrid." Madrid has seen enormous changes since Madame D'Aulnoy's visit, but its people are as devoted as ever.

Madame D'Aulnoy
(MAH-DAHM DOLE-NWAH)

THE CITY AT THE CENTER

Most capital cities lie beside deep harbors or rivers busy with cargo ships. Some stand on hilltops from which they once fought off enemy attacks. Though Madrid was built on a high plateau, it is relatively flat. It is far from the ocean, and its main river, the Manzanares, is narrow and sluggish. Madrid developed as a major city because of its location in the middle of Spain. It provides the Spaniards with a much-needed common ground.

Spain is a nation of diverse ethnic groups. The Basques, Catalonians, and others hold proudly to their languages and traditions. Yet people from Spain's most far-flung provinces follow the roads to Madrid. In the capital city, they set aside their differences and become Madrileños. The term *Madrileño* refers to a Madrid citizen.

Manzanares (MAHN-THAH-NAH-RACE)
Basque (BASK)
Catalonian (KAT-UH-LONE-EE-UN)
Madrileño (MAH-DREE-LANE-YO)

A Basque couple

Left: A view of the
Manzanares River

Below: A
Catalonian man

With 3.5 million people, Madrid is Spain's largest city. It sprawls over 234 square miles (606 square kilometers) and seems to grow bigger with each passing year. For centuries, Spain was divided into regions called provinces. Madrid was once the capital of the province of Castile. The form of Spanish known as Castilian is Spain's official language.

Castile (KASS-TEEL)

SUNDAYS AND SAINTS

On Sunday mornings, Madrileños waken to a clamor of church bells. Most Madrileños are Roman Catholics. Madrid is a city of Catholic churches, many of them dating back to the sixteenth and seventeenth centuries. The larger churches are adorned with religious statues and paintings. As they take part in Mass, worshipers gaze upon some of the world's most glorious art treasures.

Madrid has two patron saints, San Isidro and the Virgin of Almudena. These saints are thought to be the city's special protectors. According to legend, a statue of the Virgin of Almudena was hidden in the wall of a Madrid fortification during the ninth century. Some 200 years later, a young woman called Maria the Blessed promised God that she would lay down her life if the imprisoned statue could be rescued. The wall collapsed with a thundering roar and the statue was revealed. Maria the Blessed perished in her joy. The Virgin of Almudena is a favorite saint among Madrid's teenage girls.

Madrid's Cathedral of La Almudena

The Blessing of the Animals

Every January, Madrileños bring their cats, dogs, and other pets to the Church of San Antonio Abad. Priests confer their blessings upon the yipping, mewing throng. They pray for the health and prosperity of the animals in the coming year.

San Isidro is said to have performed many miracles. He could heal the sick and make water gush from solid rock. When it was time for him to plow his fields, troops of angels descended from heaven to do the work for him.

San Isidro's feast day, May 15, begins a three-week festival in Madrid. People pour into the capital from all over Spain.

The festival is an extravaganza of processions, music, dancing, and food. It is a party to which everyone in the city has an invitation.

During the procession of San Isidro, Madrileños carry a statue of the saint through the streets of Madrid.

San Isidro (SAHN EE-SEED-ROE)
Almudena (AHL-MOO-DEH-NAH)

A Spanish guitar

Flamenco musicians in a Madrid café

CREATURES OF THE NIGHT

In many parts of Madrid, restaurants do not serve the evening meal until nine-thirty or ten. A typical dinner begins with soup, followed by fish or an egg dish. Next comes the main course of meat and vegetables. Finally, dessert is served—fruit, pastry, or a rich custard called *flan*. Madrileños dine at a leisurely pace, joking and telling stories between courses. The whole meal can stretch over three hours.

By the time dinner is over, it is nearly one in the morning. To the Madrileños, the night has barely begun. From the restaurants they move on to the taverns. There they sip wine, listen to lively guitar music, and visit with friends. Sometimes, Madrileños stop at four or five taverns, meeting friends at every one.

flamenco (FLAH-MENG-KOE
flan (FLAHN)

*Madrileños at the family table, where dinner is
served at an earlier hour than at a Madrid restaurant*

As dawn streaks the sky, the Madrileños have breakfast at side-walk cafés. A steaming mug of chocolate is the finishing touch to the long night of talk and laughter. Breakfast is over just in time for the banks and offices to open. Without pausing to rest, the Madrileños set out for work.

Clearly, Madrileños do not spend every evening out on the town. But the city is famous for its nightlife. Madrileños are often called *los gatos*, or "the cats," because they come out after the sun goes down. No one seems to know when they find time to sleep. Perhaps they catnap during the day.

Madrid's Plaza de España (Spanish Plaza) just after sunset

Specialty of the House

The dish known as *paella* originated in the Spanish province of Valencia. Today, it is a specialty in many Madrid restaurants. Paella is a rich blend of rice, chicken, and fish. Clams, mussels, and oysters are arranged on top in their half-open shells. Paella is cooked in a two-handled copper pan called a *paellera*.

Madrid's Botín is the world's oldest continuously operating restaurant.

los gatos (LOCE GAH-TOCE)
paella (PAH-EH-YAH)
paellera (PAH-EH-YEH-RAH)

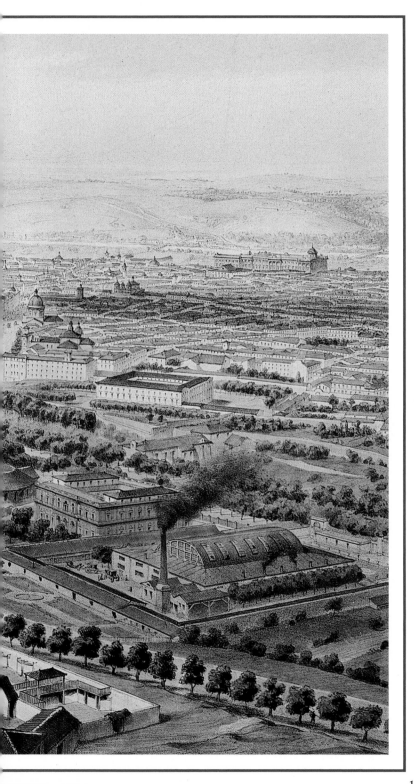

On the Plaza de la Villa in central Madrid stands an ancient stone tower. Madrileños call it the Torre de los Lujanes (Lujanes Tower). According to legend, a French king, Francis I, was imprisoned here in 1525 after his defeat in a war with Spain. The Torre de los Lujanes is one of the oldest buildings in Madrid. It is among the last remnants of Madrid's early history.

Plaza de la Villa (PLAH-THAH DEH LAH VEE-YAH)
Torre de los Lujanes
(TORE-REH DEH LOCE LOO-HAH-NACE)

FROM FORTRESS TO CAPITAL

Sometime in the ninth century A.D., Moorish people from North Africa built a fortification near the site of today's Plaza del Oriente. The Moors called their tiny walled settlement Majrit. At the time, most of Spain was in Moorish hands. Majrit was an unimportant outpost in the large territory the Moors had conquered.

The Roman Catholic people of Spain fought a long series of wars with the Moors, who were Muslims. In 1083, the Moors were finally driven out of Castile. Castile's King Alfonso VII gave Majrit, or Madrid, its first municipal charter in 1202.

For brief periods, Madrid served as the capital of Castile. But for the most part, it remained in the shadows for the next three centuries. In the meantime, Spain was amassing colonies in the New World. Ships laden with gold and silver sailed

A ninth-century battle between the Spaniards and the Moors

Plaza del Oriente
(PLAH-THAH DELL OH-REE-EN-TEH)

into Spanish ports. Spain became the richest and most powerful country on earth.

King Philip II dreamed of creating a magnificent new capital for Spain. In 1561, he chose the obscure little town of Madrid. Its central location made it an ideal site. Philip ordered an array of new churches and a magnificent palace called the Alcazar to be built. Soon Madrid was a sea of mud, bricks, and plaster as construction got underway. The turmoil may have been too much for the king. In 1563, he left Madrid for the Escorial Palace 30 miles (48 km) to the west. During his lifetime, Madrid remained a work in progress. It was a capital where the king did not even try to rule.

A Spanish treasure ship, 1590

King Philip II of Spain

Alcazar (AHL-CAH-THAR)
Escorial (EHS-KOE-REE-AHL)

THE ROYAL CAPITAL

A s Spain's fortunes rose, Madrid grew more resplendent. A series of kings held power
in the capital. Some were related to the Hapsburgs, the ruling family of Austria.
Others were Bourbons, descendants of the royal family of France. All of these kings
enhanced Madrid with churches, bridges, and public squares. The elegant Plaza Mayor,
or Grand Plaza, was completed in 1619. The plaza has been a public gathering place for
more than 300 years. After the Alcazar was destroyed by fire in 1734, a new Royal
Palace was built.

The kings made Madrid a beautiful city. But they led Spain into many
costly wars. As time passed, the Spanish people grew to resent their royal
leaders. Then, in 1808, French emperor
Napoleon Bonaparte invaded Spain.
Napoleon placed his brother Joseph on
the throne in Madrid.

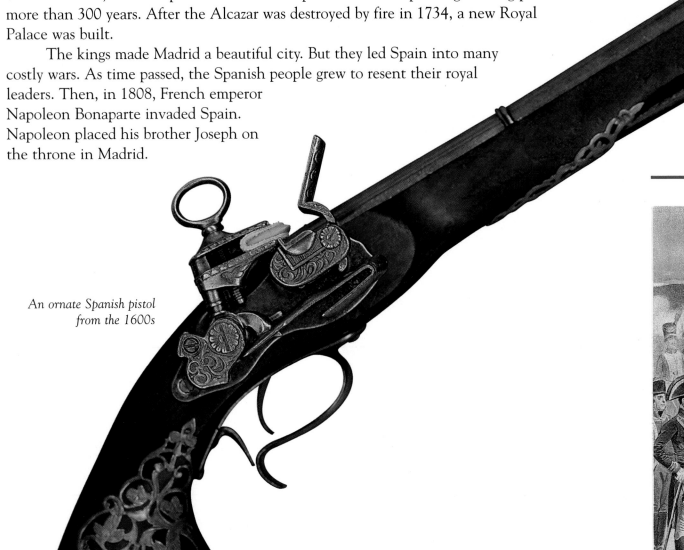

An ornate Spanish pistol
from the 1600s

Plaza Mayor (PLAH-THAH MAH-YORE)

Acts of Faith

For about 400 years, beginning in the 1100s A.D., the Roman Catholic Church carried out an inquisition against people who did not follow its teachings. Nonbelievers, or heretics, were questioned, tortured, and often put to death. Tortures under the Inquisition were known as "acts of faith." Thousands of acts of faith and executions were performed in Madrid's Plaza Mayor before the Inquisition ran its brutal course.

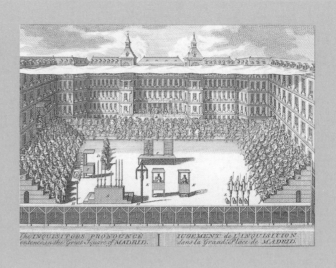

Some Spaniards supported Napoleon. They were glad to be rid of the monarchy that had ruled Spain for so long. But most of the country fought the invaders. In the hills around Madrid, peasant soldiers waged a tireless war of resistance. At last, in 1813, Spain drove out the Bonapartes and restored the monarchy. For better or for worse, the kings had returned.

At this battle in 1808, the French were defeated by a smaller Spanish force.

UPHEAVAL AND TRANSFORMATION

For more than a hundred years, one inept monarch followed another in Madrid. The people of Spain were ready for change. In 1931, King Alfonso XIII was forced to give up the throne. Spain became a republic with elected leaders. Five years later, the Communist-leaning United Front swept Spain's national elections. Calling themselves Republicans, members of the United Front promised to give real power to the Spanish people. They began by burning hundreds of churches, claiming that the priests kept the people in bondage. They murdered wealthy landholders and factory owners on the grounds that they oppressed the poor.

In the midst of this chaos, a Spanish army general named Francisco Franco launched a rebellion in 1936. Franco proclaimed himself leader of the Nationalist movement and set out to overthrow the Republicans. For nearly three years, Spain was wracked by a terrible civil war. More than a million people lost their lives in the Spanish Civil War.

King Alfonso XIII of Spain

The Great Caudillo

As dictator of Spain, Francisco Franco (1892–1975) called himself *el caudillo*, or "the leader." Franco, who became an army general at the age of thirty-four, was also called *generalissimo, or* "the supreme general." As premier of Spain, Franco wielded tremendous power. He used the military to maintain tight control over the country.

el caudillo (ELL COW-DEE-YO)
generalissimo (HEN-EH-RAH-LEE-SEE-MOE)
Alfonso (AHL-FON-SO)
Francisco Franco (FRAHN-THEECE-KOE FRAHN-KOH)

This street battle took place in Madrid during the 1936–1939 Spanish Civil War.

Madrileños give the Nationalist salute to this tank crew of Franco's after the surrender of Madrid.

This illustration on the front page of La Tribuna Illustrata shows Franco's victorious army entering Madrid.

LA TRIBUNA ILLUSTRATA

Le magnifiche Fanterie della Spagna Nazionale e i prodi Legionari d'Italia entrano a Madrid.

Through most of the war, Madrid was in Republican hands. For 28 months, with support from Fascist dictators Adolf Hitler and Benito Mussolini, Franco's Nationalist forces held the city under siege. Food supplies fell dangerously low. Madrileños were issued 2 ounces (57 grams) of rice a day. Hundreds of people died of starvation and disease.

On March 28, 1939, Nationalist troops stormed the weakened capital. The fall of Madrid brought

Prince Juan Carlos took the throne at the death of Franco in 1975.

Spanish coins bearing the portrait of Juan Carlos

Franco to power and ushered Spain into a new era. Franco was an absolute dictator. In the 1940s and 1950s, he suppressed free speech and demanded total loyalty. During the 1960s, however, his regime became somewhat more relaxed. Franco encouraged construction and industry. By the time he died in 1975, Spain enjoyed prosperity as a modern nation.

Before his death, Franco appointed Prince Juan Carlos to be his successor. Juan Carlos, the grandson of Alfonso XIII, took the throne in 1975. Once again, a monarch rules in Madrid.

Juan Carlos
(̲HWAHN KAHR-ʟᴏᴄᴇ)

AT PLAY

During the San Isidro Festival, Madrileños enjoy a series of lively operettas known as *zarzuelas*. The zarzuelas are thin on plot but rich with singing and dancing. Most zarzuelas praise life in Madrid. Madrileños find many other ways to celebrate their city as well—through music, art, and recreation.

zarzuela (THAHR-THWAY-LAH)

THE JOY OF MUSIC

Madrid's royal court encouraged all of the fine arts. During the seventeenth and eighteenth centuries, some of the best musicians in Europe visited Madrid. They played at royal ceremonies and composed pieces in honor of the kings. Among the most famous composers who spent time in Madrid were two Italians, Domenico Scarlatti (1685–1757) and Luigi Boccherini (1743–1805). They both wrote chamber music. Chamber music is played by small ensembles of instruments such as violins, cellos, flutes, and harpsichords.

The music of many ethnic traditions was heard on the streets of Madrid in the age of the kings. There were Gypsy dances, Jewish holiday songs, and Arab love chants. Today, Madrid's popular music is flavored with all these ingredients. But young Madrileños prefer rock music. They import it from other countries and also create their own.

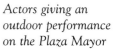

Actors giving an outdoor performance on the Plaza Mayor

This old engraving shows
two Spanish gypsy girls playing
a guitar and a tambourine.

A flute such as those used in
some chamber music ensenbles

Domenico Scarlatti (DOE-MEN-EE-KOE SCAR-LAH-TEE)
Luigi Boccherini (LOO-EE-GEE BOAK-KEH-REE-NEE)

Many of Madrid's night-clubs are vibrant with strumming guitars and chattering castanets. This is *flamenco*, a musical form unique to Spain. Flamenco originated in the province of Andalusia, but it has a strong following in Madrid. The music is both sung and danced. Some flamenco songs are achingly sad. They deal with broken dreams, partings, and death. Others are festive songs about dancing and young love.

By tradition, men and women dance flamenco in very different ways. Men perform fast, complicated steps, tapping their toes and clicking their heels. Female dancers move more smoothly, with elegance and grace.

Castanets

This young Madrid girl is wearing a traditional Spanish outfit.

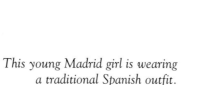

castanets (KAST-UH-NETS)
flamenco (FLAH-MENG-koe)
Andalusia (AN-DUH-LOOZ-YUH)

This lace mantilla is attached to an elegant headpiece with a comb that is anchored in a dancer's hair.

Dancers at a flamenco fiesta

A PICTURE'S WORTH A THOUSAND WORDS

The story of Don Quixote is familiar all over the world. Dressed in rusty armor, Don Quixote rides about the Spanish countryside on a stumbling nag. Beside him is his faithful squire, Sancho Panza, mounted on a donkey. In the most famous episode, Don Quixote attacks a windmill with his lance, mistaking it for a dangerous giant. Don Quixote, the comical knight who longs to right the world's wrongs, is one of the most beloved characters in literature. The novel *Don Quixote* was written by Miguel de Cervantes (1542–1616), who spent much of his life in Madrid.

A statue of Don Quixote

An illustration from Don Quixote *titled "After being beaten by the muleteers, he is taken home by Sancho Panza."*

Though Madrid has been home to many outstanding writers, the city is best known as a haven for painters. Madrid's renowned museum, El Prado, displays some of Europe's greatest art treasures. The museum is a must for every visitor who sets foot in the city. Some Madrileños drop by the museum every few weeks to visit their favorite paintings.

Above: A statue of Cervantes in the Plaza de España

Left: Miguel de Cervantes, author of Don Quixote

Don Quixote (DOAN kee-HOE-teh)
Sancho Panza (SAHN-choh PAHN-thah)
Miguel de Cervantes (MEE-GALE deh thair-VAHN-tace)
El Prado (ELL PRAH-doe)
Plaza de España (PLAH-thah deh ess-PAHN-yah)

Highlighted at El Prado is the work of three great Spanish artists: El Greco, Velázquez, and Goya. The artist known as El Greco was born Domenikos Theotokopoulos (1541–1614). He grew up on the Greek island of Crete, and reached Madrid around 1570. His name must have mystified the Spaniards, for they simply called him *El Greco,* or "the Greek." El Greco did some fine painting in the capital, but settled in Toledo, about 40 miles (64 km) to the south. Most of El Greco's paintings are religious works or portraits.

Diego Velázquez (1599–1660) began his career by painting pictures to decorate churches. Later, he worked at court in Madrid, doing portraits of the royal family.

Velázquez also rendered many scenes of ordinary life. He liked to paint kitchen scenes such as *Old Woman Frying Eggs.*

Madrid's renowned art museum, El Prado

The Repentant Magdalene, *by El Greco*

Portrait of Camillo Astalli, *by Velázquez*

El Greco's Annunciation

El Greco (ELL-GREH-KOE)
Domenikos Theotokopoulas
(DOE-MEN-IH-KOCE THAY-OH-TOE-
KOE-POO-LOCE)
Diego Velázquez
(DEE-AY-GO VEH-LAHSS-KAYTH)

Miracles on the Ceiling

In 1798, Francisco Goya was commissioned to create frescoes on the ceiling of Madrid's Chapel of San Antonio de la Florida. Goya depicted St. Anthony performing miracles amid a crowd of poor people. Many nobles and priests were offended by his realistic portrayal of human suffering. Today, art lovers travel from all over the world to view Goya's frescoes.

Like Velázquez, Francisco Goya (1746–1828) served as a court painter in Madrid. He painted portraits of several of the Spanish monarchs and of Joseph Bonaparte. Most court painters tried to please the royals by making them look handsome, powerful, and wise. But Goya was not afraid to paint the kings and queens as he really saw them. His portraits sometimes revealed the monarchs as cruel or even foolish. Goya's honesty finally got him into so much trouble that he had to leave Spain forever.

Francisco Goya (FRAHN-THEECE-KOE GO-YAH)
tertulia (TARE-TOO-LEE-AH)
San Antonio de la Florida
(SAHN AHN-TOE-NEE-OH DEH LAH FLOE-REE-DAH)

The Third of May, 1808, *by Goya*

A street painter near the Puerta del Sol

A ticket to the Prado Museum

By long tradition, writers and artists have always loved to gather at cafés and discuss their work. In Spain, these lively discussion groups are called *tertulias*. Under the regime of Francisco Franco, most tertulias were suppressed. Writers and artists did not dare to express themselves freely. Since Franco's death, however, the arts have made a dramatic comeback in Madrid. Once again, tertulias flourish. Talking and debating, Madrileños watch the long night turn to morning.

"OLÉ! OLÉ!"

Most foreign visitors to Madrid are repelled by the thought of bullfighting. Yet nearly every tourist attends the bullfights at least once to learn what they are really like. American writer Ernest Hemingway became fascinated with bullfighting when he lived in Spain during the 1920s. "[The bullfight] is not an equal contest or an attempt at an equal contest between a bull and a man," Hemingway explained. "Rather it is a tragedy, the death of the bull, which is played more or less well by the bull and the man involved, and in which there is danger for the man but certain death for the bull."

The bullfight is a spectacle of stirring music and brightly colored costumes. The bullfighter, or *matador*, swirls his red cape, teasing the bull into an attack. When the matador makes an especially bold or graceful move, the crowd shouts "Olé! Olé!" Most bullfights are held on Sunday afternoons and include six separate contests. During the San Isidro Festival in May, Madrileños can attend bullfights nearly every day for three weeks.

olé (OH-LAY)
matador (MAH-TAH-DORE)
Barcelona (BAR-SEH-LONE-UH)

This statue of a bullfighter stands outside Madrid's bullfight arena, Plaza de Toros de Las Ventas.

Trophies for the Victor

After the matador kills the bull, several judges rate his performance. As trophies, the judges award the matador parts of the creature he has slain. The matador may receive one or both of the bull's ears, the ears and the tail, or, on rare occasions, one of the hoofs.

A bullfighter in the ring at the Plaza de Toros de las Ventas

The San Isidro Festival sometimes hosts a soccer competition between Madrid and Barcelona. The long-standing rivalry between the two cities heightens the excitement of this major event. Soccer is immensely popular in Madrid, as it is throughout Spain. Boys and girls in Madrid follow soccer stars the way children in the United States follow basketball heroes.

A student playing soccer at University City

HEAVEN

Madrileños have a saying: "From Madrid to Heaven, and in Heaven a little window from which to look at Madrid." In other words, Paradise would be flawed for the Madrileños if they couldn't gaze upon their beloved city. Exploring the churches, museums, and plazas of Madrid, the visitor may begin to understand what the old saying means.

OUT ON THE FRINGES

During the second half of the twentieth century, Madrid more than doubled in population. The city spread wider and wider, engulfing much of the surrounding countryside. Madrid's newest sections bristle with high-rise apartments and office buildings. People flock to shopping malls instead of strolling in open-air plazas. Traffic speeds endlessly along a maze of superhighways.

If this is your first glimpse of Madrid, you may think it is no different from any other congested modern city. But as you move toward the city's older areas, you catch glimpses of Madrid's unique character. Old Madrid is a city of broad, tree-lined boulevards. Among them is the Paseo de la Castellana, an elegant thoroughfare lined with restaurants, theaters, and government ministries. Another boule-

Getting around in Madrid

Traffic in Madrid is a nightmare, but fortunately it is possible to get around without a car. Madrid's subway system, the Metro, began operation in 1921. The city also has extensive bus lines. Taxis are fairly inexpensive, and they seem to be everywhere. Madrid has twice as many cabs per person as does New York City.

vard, the Gran Via, is Madrid's premier shopping street. At the far end of the Gran Via is the Plaza de España (Spanish Plaza). The plaza is graced by bronze statues of Don Quixote and his faithful squire Sancho Panza. Looming above the plaza is Torre de Madrid (Madrid Tower), one of the loftiest skyscrapers in Europe.

Paseo de la Castellana
(PAH-SEH-OH DEH LAH CASS-TEH-YAH-NAH)
Gran Via (GRAHN VEE-UH)
Torre de Madrid (TORE-REH DEH MAH-DREED)

Above: The Plaza de España

Left: The Gran Via

Right: A young Madrileño

The University of Madrid stands in University City on Madrid's northwestern edge. During the Spanish Civil War of 1936–1939, University City was nearly destroyed by bombs. Today, most of the university buildings are modern in design. The university area has many lively cafés where tertulias abound.

Retiro Park was once the playground of the Spanish kings. Today, it is a playground for all of Madrid. The park has something for everyone—bicycle trails, fountains, a boating pond, and a small zoo. Within the park, the Botanical Garden displays plants and trees from around the world.

Students on a field trip to Retiro Park's Botanical Garden

Spanish schoolgirls at Retiro Park

The Crystal Palace in Retiro Park

The park is dotted with statues and monuments, most of them honoring kings and military heroes. One statue is different. It shows a grinning ghoul with horns and a long tail. It is the only public statue in the world that represents Satan.

Retiro (REH-TEE-ROE)

HEADING DOWNTOWN

Madrid's Royal Palace was built in 1738 on the site of the old Alcazar. The royal family has not lived in the palace since 1931. (Juan Carlos and his wife Sofia live in the smaller Zarzuela Palace outside Madrid.) The Royal Palace has more than 1,800 rooms, a handful of which are open to the public. Visitors can walk through state living quarters, the reception salon, and the Royal Pharmacy. At the Royal Pharmacy, medicines were once concocted and handed out free to those in need. Many of these medicines were made from herbs grown in the Royal Gardens on the palace grounds.

Sofia (SO-FEE-AH)

Far left: The Royal Palace
Above: An interior view of the Royal Palace
Left: Two Spanish schoolgirls with popsicles

49

The Barrios Bajos, the poor neighborhoods of Madrid, are a stunning contrast to the Royal Palace. For centuries, the city's poorest families lived here in tiny, crowded houses on a maze of narrow streets. Many of Madrid's poor residents have now left the Barrios Bajos and live in new low-income housing on the outskirts of the city. A colorful feature of the Barrios Bajos is El Rastro, a vast flea market that reaches over several blocks. During the summer, El Rastro stays open until daybreak.

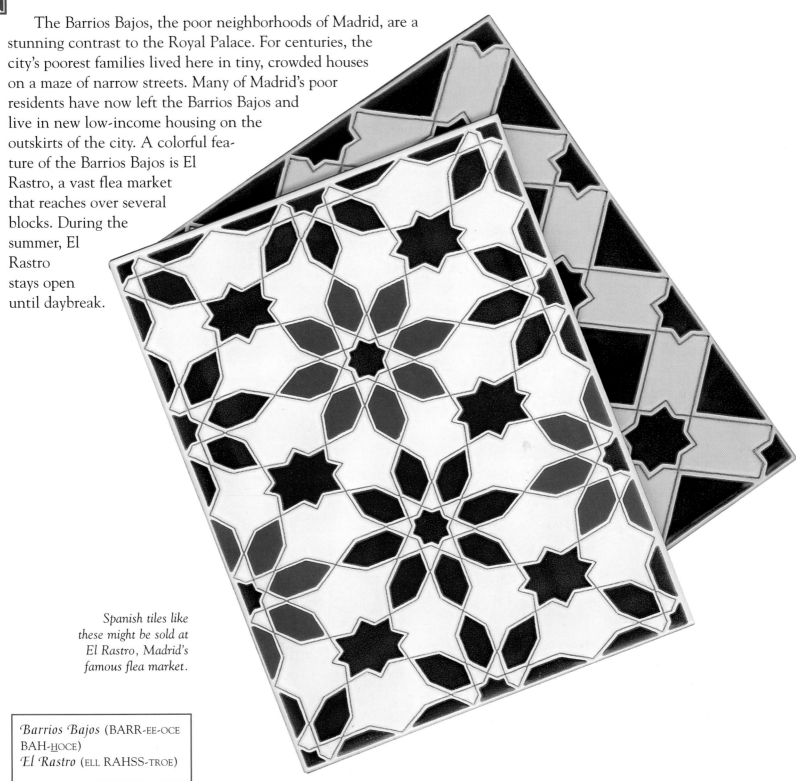

Spanish tiles like these might be sold at El Rastro, Madrid's famous flea market.

Barrios Bajos (BARR-ee-oce BAH-hoce)
El Rastro (ELL RAHSS-troe)

This El Rastro vendor
has three kittens to sell.

The Municipal Museum
is a good place to learn about
Madrid's long history.
Exhibits cover the archaeolo-
gy of the region, the Moorish
conquest, and Madrid in
Spain's "golden age."
Exquisite tapestries depict
Madrid life in the eighteenth
century. Another display
shows models of the Plaza
Mayor at several historic
periods.

A view of El Rastro

The Alcala Gate is a stately arched gateway built in the late eighteenth century. Nearby stands the Prado Museum, one of the foremost art museums in the world. The Prado is housed in a former eighteenth-century palace. Its grand halls are a magnificent setting for paintings by Goya, Velázquez, and other masters. The Prado's most important work is *The Handmaidens*, a painting by Velázquez.

The Prado displays art from the fifteenth through the nineteenth centuries. Twentieth-century painting and sculpture are on exhibit at the Queen Sophia National Museum of Art. This modern-art museum is housed in what was once Madrid's General Hospital, though the museum was modernized in 1992. Its collections include work by such twentieth-century Spanish greats as Salvador Dalí and Pablo Picasso. Picasso's stunning antiwar painting, *Guernica*, is among the museum's treasures.

The Alcala Gate

Pilgrimage of a Painting

Picasso's painting *Guernica* depicts the 1937 bombing of a Spanish village by supporters of Francisco Franco. When the war was over, Franco would not permit the painting to be displayed in Spain. Until Franco's death, *Guernica* hung in New York's Museum of Modern Art. Now, at last, it can be seen in Madrid, a grim reminder of the horrors of war.

Visitors at the Prado Museum

Alcala (AHL-KAH-LAH)
Guernica (GWEHR-NEE-KAH)

These girls are students at University City in Madrid.

THE HEART OF THE CITY

Under Spain's Bourbon kings, the Plaza Mayor was the center of Madrid. Crowds gathered on the plaza to watch bullfights, jousting tournaments, and executions. The Plaza Mayor no longer hosts these public spectacles, but it is still a favorite place for people to gather. During the summer, Madrileños stroll the park from sunset to dawn.

The Plaza Mayor is an immense rectangle paved with cobblestones. Its shorter side is the length of a football field. Along the edges of the plaza run a series of columned porticoes. Shaded from the sun, vendors sell leather goods, jewelry, coins, stamps, and snacks. The plaza is surrounded by four- and five-story houses and apartment buildings, each with several balconies. People love to sit on their balconies and survey the plaza below.

This statue of Felipe III stands in the Plaza Mayor.

Sometimes the strains of guitars float up from the street as a band of student musicians wanders by.

Compared with the Plaza Mayor, the Puerta del Sol is small and rather dingy. But Madrileños still

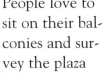

A child on the Plaza Mayor

regard it as the very center of their city and their nation. The clock on the Puerta del Sol is a beloved city landmark. Day by day, it ticks away the time until Madrileños gather to ring in the New Year. Once again, they will pack the plaza and pop grapes into their mouths, one for each stroke of midnight.

FAMOUS LANDMARKS

Above: The Museo Municipal (Municipal Museum), once a seventeenth-century hospital, is now a historical museum.

Left: Plaza Mayor

Plaza Mayor
Madrid's most important plaza for more than 300 years. The Plaza Mayor is surrounded by arcades where vendors sell their wares. Beneath the plaza is a maze of underground shops and taverns.

Puerta del Sol
Smaller plaza that Madrileños regard as the center of their city and nation. By tradition, crowds gather here to welcome in the New Year.

Prado Museum
One of the finest art museums in the world. The Prado displays European works created between 1500 and 1900. The museum specializes in paintings by the Spanish masters El Greco, Velázquez, and Goya.

Queen Sophia National Museum of Art
Museum that features art of the twentieth century. It displays paintings by Juan Miró, Salvador Dalí, and Pablo Picasso, among others. Picasso's painting *Guernica* is part of its collection.

Royal Palace
Palace inhabited by Spanish monarchs from 1738 to 1931. Franco used it for state ceremonies but never lived here. The palace has more than 1,800 rooms, several of which are now open to the public.

Royal Tapestry Factory
Weaving operation dating to the late 1700s. Tapestries are based on sketches or "cartoons," many of them originally drawn by the painter Goya. Some weavers spend a lifetime creating the same picture over and over again.

A detail of the ceiling fresco painted by Goya at San Antonio de la Florida

Retiro Park

The plaza in front of the Royal Palace

Chapel of San Antonio de la Florida

Chapel where Goya painted his famous frescoes in 1798. The ceiling shows a crowd of ordinary people gathered around St. Anthony. After Goya died in exile, his bones were returned to Madrid and buried in this chapel.

Bullfighting Museum

Museum adjoining Madrid's main bullfighting stadium (Plaza de Toros de la Ventas). On exhibit are photographs, bullfight programs and posters, and statues of famous matadors.

Municipal Museum

Museum that traces the history of Madrid. It tells the city's story through archaeological exhibits, paintings, photos, tapestries, and scale models of the Plaza Mayor.

Retiro Park

The largest park in Madrid. Covering 350 acres (142 ha), it was formerly a recreation ground for the royal family. Today, the park contains a zoo, a botanical garden, and miles of paths for hiking and bicycling. Within the park is the Army Museum, containing swords, armor, and relics from early Spanish expeditions to the New World.

Puerta de Toledo

City gate built by Joseph Bonaparte. The gate is a splendid arch of triumph designed for the Emperor Napoleon. The gate later became a symbol of Spain's loyalty to its Bourbon kings.

Naval Museum

Museum that documents the history of Spanish seafaring. The most cherished exhibit is a map of the New World drawn by the first mate on Columbus's flagship, the *Santa Maria*.

El Rastro

Large flea market that covers several blocks. El Rastro is famous for its great bargains and clever pickpockets.

FAST FACTS

POPULATION (1995)   3,123,317

AREA   234 square miles (606 sq km)

ALTITUDE   2,150 feet (655 m) above sea level

LOCATION Madrid is located on a broad, high plateau in central Spain. It serves as Spain's capital city.

CLIMATE Madrid has a warm, dry climate with relatively little rainfall. January temperatures average 40 degrees Fahrenheit (4.4° Celsius). Temperatures in July climb to 74 degrees Fahrenheit (23° Celsius), though on especially hot summer days, temperatures can rise to 104 degrees Fahrenheit (40° Celsius)

ECONOMY Because Madrid is the capital of Spain, many Madrileños work in government service. The city and surrounding suburbs also have a variety of thriving industries. Madrid's factories produce automobiles, clothing, leather goods, and an assortment of other products.

CHRONOLOGY

9th century A.D.
Moors from North Africa establish Majrit, a fortified outpost at the site of today's Plaza del Oriente.

1083
The Moors are driven out of the province of Castile.

1202
King Alfonso VII of Spain gives Madrid its first municipal charter.

1492
The Moors are expelled from Spain; Christopher Columbus reaches the Caribbean and launches Spain's empire in the New World.

1525
Francis I of France is imprisoned in Madrid's Lujanes Tower.

1561
King Philip II selects Madrid to be Spain's new capital.

1588
Great Britain destroys Spain's main fleet, the Spanish Armada.

1619
The Plaza Mayor is completed in Madrid.

1738
The Royal Palace is completed.

1798
Goya paints frescoes on the ceiling of San Antonio de la Florida.

1808
Napoleon invades Spain and puts his brother Joseph Bonaparte on the throne in Madrid.

1812
Napoleon is overthrown and Joseph Bonaparte is driven out of Spain.

1870–1875
Spain establishes a short-lived republic.

*A view of Retiro Park's
Botanical Garden*

1921
Madrid's subway system, the Metro, opens.

1931
King Alfonso XIII is pressured to give up the throne; Spain again establishes a republic.

1936
Communists win Spanish elections; Spanish Civil War begins.

1939
Civil War ends when Madrid falls to General Francisco Franco; Franco becomes dictator of Spain.

1975
Franco dies; Spanish monarchy is restored under Juan Carlos I.

1991
Mideast Peace Conference meets at Madrid's Royal Palace.

MADRID

| A | B | C | D | E | F | G | H | I | J | K |

Chapel
of San Antonio
de la Florida

Torre
de Madrid

Municipal
Museum

BOURBON MADRID

Paseo de la Castellana

Plaza
de España

Gran Via

Alcala
Gate

OLD MADRID

Royal
Palace

Plaza
del Oriente

Puerta
del Sol

Retiro
Park

Alcazar
Palace

Naval
Museum

Plaza
Mayor

Zoological
Park

Torre
de los Lujanes

Catedral
de San Isidro

Prado
Museum

Manzanares

Plaza
de la Villa

El Rastro

Queen Sophia National
Museum of Art

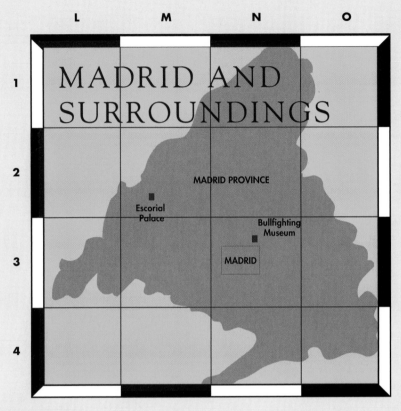

MADRID AND SURROUNDINGS

L M N O

1
2
3
4

MADRID PROVINCE

Escorial
Palace

Bullfighting
Museum

MADRID

Municipal Museum	F2
Naval Museum	G,H 5
Old Madrid	D4
Paseo de la Castellana	I 1,2
Plaza de la Villa	C6
Plaza de España	D3
Plaza del Oriente	D4
Plaza Mayor	D5
Prado Museum	H 5,6
Puerta del Sol	E5
Queen Sophia National Museum of Art	G,H 7
Retiro Park	I,J,K 4,5,6
Royal Palace	C 4,5
Torre de los Lujanes	C6
Torre de Madrid	D3
Zoological Park	K5

GLOSSARY

amass: Collect, hoard

confer: Grant

converge: Join together

enhance: Make more attractive

fresco: Painting done on the wet plaster of a wall or ceiling

harpsichord: Eighteenth-century musical instrument similar to a piano

inept: Incompetent, unable to perform well

inscribed: Written in a lasting form, such as carving in stone

jousting: Medieval sport in which mounted knights charged each other with lances

monarch: Royal ruler

paella: Dish of rice, chicken, and seafood popular in Spain

premier: Leading, foremost

regime: Ruling government

remnant: Remaining trace, relic

resplendent: Magnificent, dazzling

sluggish: Slow, lacking in energy

successor: Person who takes over an office or role

Picture Identifications

Cover: Retiro Park details; boys with soccer ball
Page 1: A group of Spanish cousins
Pages 4–5: Pedestrians in Puerto del Sol
Pages 8–9: Students on the campus, University City
Pages 18–19: Madrid, with its old bullring in the foreground, as it looked in 1854
Pages 28–29: Boating on the Retiro Park lake
Pages 42–43: Madrid's ornate post office, often called "Our Lady of the Posts" because it looks like a cathedral

INDEX

TO FIND OUT MORE

BOOKS

Biggs, Betsey. *Kidding Around Spain*. Santa Fe., N.M.: John Muir Publications, 1991.

Chambers, Catherine. *Spain*. Country Topics for Craft Projects. Danbury, Conn.: Franklin Watts, 1993.

De Cervantes, Miguel. *Don Quixote*. Cambridge, Mass.: Candlewick Press, 1993. (A version for young people)

Fodor's Spain '99. New York: Fodor's Travel Publications, Inc., 1998.

Katz, William Loren and Marc Crawford. *The Lincoln Brigade*. New York: Atheneum, 1989. (A book for young people about the Spanish Civil War and the group of Americans who fought in it against Franco)

Llombart, Felipe Vicente Garin. *Treasures of the Prado*. New York: Abbeville Press, Inc., 1994.

Loewen, Nancy and Judith A. Ahlstrom. *Food in Spain*. Vero Beach, Fla.: Rourke Publications, Inc., 1991.

Lye, Keith. *Passport to Spain*. Danbury, Conn.: Franklin Watts, 1997.

Mason, Antony. *Picasso*. Famous Artists. New York: Barrons Juveniles, 1995.

Porter, Darwin and Danforth Prince. *Frommer's Barcelona, Madrid, and Seville: The Guide to Spain's Most Exciting Cities*. New York: Macmillan Travel, 1997.

Wright, Patricia. *Goya*. Eyewitness Art. DK Publishing, 1993.

ONLINE SITES

Madrid
http://www.spaintour.com/madrid.htm
Tons of information on the history and contemporary life of Spain's capital city: shopping, museums, music, sports, food, and all the sights.

Madrid, Spain
http://cityguide.lycos.com/europe/spain/ESPMadrid.html
Great starting point for links to sites about Madrid, including news, weather, culture, history, and entertainment.

Museo Thyssen Bornemisza
http://www.offcampus.es/thyssen/homepage-eng.html
Visit one of Madrid's most important museums: guided tours, general information, and activities.

Prado Museum
http://museoprado.mcu.es/prado/html/ihome.html
History of the world-famous museum, as well as news, upcoming events, and guided tours. See paintings by Goya, Velázquez, and others.

Real Madrid Soccer
http://www.yrl.co.uk/~gonzalo/rm/rm_english.html
Everything you could want to know about Madrid's most famous soccer team.

Useful Guide to Madrid
http://malika.iem.csic.es/~grant/madi.html
Guides, maps, newspapers, and hundreds of links.

U.S. Embassy in Madrid
http://www.embusa.es/indexbis.html
Information about the embassy, current topics, business, education, and tourism.

ABOUT THE AUTHOR

Deborah Kent grew up in Little Falls, New Jersey, and received a B.A. in English from Oberlin College. She earned a master's degree from Smith College School for Social Work. After working for four years at the University Settlement House in New York City, she moved to San Miguel de Allende in central Mexico. There she wrote her first young-adult novel, *Belonging*.